PROFILES

Martin Luther King

Nigel Richardson

Illustrated by
Tammy Wong

Evans Brothers Limited

Published by Evans Brothers Limited
2A Portman Mansions
Chiltern Street
London W1M 1LE

First published in Great Britain in 1983 by
Hamish Hamilton Children's Books

© Nigel Richardson (text) 1983

© Tammy Wong (illustrations) 1983

All Rights Reserved. No part of this publication may be reproduced, stored in a retrieval system or transmitted in any form or by any means, electronic, mechanical, photocopying, recording or otherwise, without prior permission of Evans Brothers Limited.

Reprinted 1984, 1987, 1992 (twice)

Typeset by Pioneer
Printed by Stephens & George Ltd,
South Wales, Great Britain.
Tel: 0685 5351

ISBN 0 237 60007 2

Titles in this series

Ian Botham	0 237 60030 7	Bob Geldof	0 237 60031 5
Edith Cavell	0 237 60020 X	Amy Johnson	0 237 60032 3
Marie Curie	0 237 60024 2	Helen Keller	0 237 60016 1
Roald Dahl	0 237 60010 2	John F. Kennedy	0 237 60029 3
Thomas Edison	0 237 60006 4	Florence Nightingale	0 237 60018 8
Alexander Fleming	0 237 60013 7	Emmeline Pankhurst	0 237 60019 6
John Lennon	0 237 60021 8	Anna Pavlova	0 237 60002 1
Martin Luther King	0 237 60007 2	Pope John Paul II	0 237 60005 6
Nelson Mandela	0 237 60026 9	Prince Philip	0 237 60012 9
Bob Marley	0 237 60017 X	Queen Elizabeth II	0 237 60302 0
Mother Teresa	0 237 60008 0	Queen Elizabeth the Queen Mother	0 237 60009 9
Margot Fonteyn	0 237 60033 1		
Anne Frank	0 237 60015 3	Queen Victoria	0 237 60001 3
Elizabeth Fry	0 237 60028 5	Viv Richards	0 237 60027 7
Gandhi	0 237 60011 0	Margaret Thatcher	0 237 60003 X
Indira Gandhi	0 237 60025 0		

Contents

1	UNTIL THE DAY I DIE	7
2	AMAZING PATIENCE	11
3	THE MOST PECULIAR CHILD	17
4	A VERY BRIGHT YOUNG MAN	20
5	TIRED OF BEING KICKED ABOUT	26
6	GOD SPOKE FROM WASHINGTON	31
7	THE TIME HAS COME	35
8	JUSTICE TOO LONG DELAYED	40
9	I HAVE A DREAM	45
10	WE MUST STAND UP	49
11	I'VE SEEN THE PROMISED LAND	54
12	A LIFE SERVING OTHERS	59
	Important events in the life of Dr Martin Luther King	63

1 'Until the day I die'

One afternoon in 1935 a six-year-old boy came home from school and ran across the road outside his home to play with two of his friends. His family called him 'Mike' or 'M.L.', but he was later to be known as Martin Luther King. He was the son of a minister at the local Baptist church in Atlanta, Georgia, a bustling city in the south-east corner of the United States.

The King family was greatly respected in Atlanta. Martin's grandfather had founded the church, and his father was an important figure in the local community. His friends were the two children of the local grocer, and he had played with them ever since he could remember, flying kites and model planes, riding bicycles or practising baseball and basketball in the back yard. But they and Martin had now started at different schools and Martin was anxious to find out what their school was like compared with his own.

He was surprised when their mother told him that the boys could not play with him any more. He asked her why, but at first she just made excuses, saying the boys were too busy. Martin was puzzled and asked her again for the reason. Finally, she told him. They were white, and he was black, and now that the children had all reached school age, they must go their separate ways. They would never be allowed to play with Martin again.

'None of us had seriously thought anything about white children being different,' Martin recalled later. Hurt and confused, he had run home to his mother and

Martin Luther King's father was a minister in the Baptist church in Atlanta, Georgia

asked her to explain. 'Don't let this thing worry you,' she told him. 'Don't let it make you feel you are not as good as white people. You are as good as anyone else, and don't you forget it.' But from that day onwards, Martin gradually learned how differently black and white people were treated.

Two years later, when he was eight, his father took him out one day to buy a pair of shoes. They sat down near the front of the shop. A white assistant came over to them and said 'I'll be happy to serve you if you'll just come to those seats at the back.' 'Why?' asked Martin's father. 'There's nothing wrong with these seats.' 'Sorry,' said the assistant, 'but you'll have to go back there.

These seats are for whites only.' 'We'll either buy shoes sitting here,' replied Daddy King, 'or we won't buy shoes at all.' Both father and son walked out of the shop. 'It was probably the first time I had seen Daddy so furious,' remembered Martin later. 'I remember him muttering "I don't care how long I have to live with this system, I am never going to accept it. I'll oppose it until the day I die".'

As he got older Martin gradually learned more about the differences between black and white. Policemen would always refer scornfully to a young negro as 'boy' or an elderly one as 'uncle'. Once, when a traffic policeman yelled at his father 'Boy, what d'you mean running across the road against that Stop sign?' Daddy King replied politely 'I'm a man. That's a boy there,' and he pointed to Martin beside him. 'I'm Reverend King,' he said proudly. Daddy King insisted on being treated politely by whites, but he knew that black people less well-known than he could command no respect at all.

Martin also noticed how bus drivers yelled 'Nigger' at local black students. It was a way of being rude to them. When he was eleven, a white woman walked up to him in a department store and slapped his face. He had never seen her before. 'The little nigger stepped on my foot,' she explained. No-one criticised her. Martin learned that black children not only had to go to separate schools, but that their parents were expected to move back from the best seats at the front of local buses if white people got on. His father refused to ride on them as a result. It also became clear to Martin that many of the top jobs in the city could be held only by whites.

Martin was learning the bitter lesson that all black people of his age then had to learn — that negroes in the South were treated as second-class citizens just because of the colour of their skin. It was a lesson that was to shape the whole course of his future life.

2 'Amazing Patience'

Racial discrimination (treating blacks differently from whites) and segregation (keeping them separate from whites) went back a long way in American history. Over 300 years before Martin Luther King was born, the first black slaves were brought from West Africa to America and the West Indies to work in the hot sun, growing sugar, tobacco and cotton in fields called plantations. They had no choice; they were kidnapped from their homes by men with guns and herded on to ships. On the journey they were kept like animals in the ship's hold below deck. It was dark and dirty and they were overcrowded and hungry. They had no idea where they were going or what would become of them. If they fell ill, they were sometimes thrown overboard and left to drown so that their disease would not spread to other slaves or to the white men who formed the crew.

Once in America, these slaves had no legal rights at all. White men could buy and sell them like pieces of meat or furniture. They were taken off the ships, handcuffed and roped together, and herded into the local market for inspection. White men came looking for strong plantation workers, and their wives tried to find servants who would do all the housework. They had to put up with insulting comments, and they could be prodded and stripped of all their clothes for a thorough examination. Families were split up. A mother could be sold to one buyer while her daughter was sold to another who lived hundreds of kilometres

Slaves working on a plantation

away. They would never see each other again.

Many people realised that this slave trade was wrong. Laws were passed in both Britain and America in 1807−8 to make it illegal, but an adventurous sea-captain could still dodge the naval patrols and make a lot of money out of it. By 1830 a really fit male slave might sell for £700. Some owners treated their slaves well, but others beat them cruelly. Sometimes slaves were even killed by their owners, but few owners were ever punished for their death. Some slaves tried to flee to the Northern states where there was no slavery, but the American government said that they must be sent back to their masters. Others rebelled against their owners, though the revolts were put down with great cruelty.

Slavery never spread to the Northern states because the climate there was cooler and the main slave crops like tobacco would not grow there. In the years after 1820, however, the new American nation began to spread into the huge areas of land to the west of the Atlantic coast, and many new states joined the original thirteen which had broken away from England in 1783. This led to an important question — were the new states to be allowed to have slaves or not? The South said yes, the North said no. Each side wanted the West to become like itself. At the same time, a group of whites in the North began to spread the idea that slavery was wrong. This group was known as the Abolitionists — those wanting to abolish slavery.

The whites in the South saw the Abolitionists as a threat to the whole Southern way of life. Perhaps they would even want to make blacks equal with whites. When Abraham Lincoln, a man known to support the end of slavery, was elected President of the United States in 1860, eleven Southern states (including Georgia, Martin Luther King's home state) broke away from the rest and formed their own government. A terrible civil war followed, which lasted for four years and ended in the complete defeat of the South.

During the war the government in the North declared that all slaves were now free. In 1865 it declared that slavery was banned and that the right to vote would no longer depend on the colour of a man's skin. The blacks believed that they would now win

Abraham Lincoln

equality. But the American government was in Washington, a long way from places like Georgia. Although in theory the central government in Washington could over-rule laws passed by individual states, in practice it soon became busy with other problems. Whites took power in each Southern state and quickly introduced laws which would keep the blacks permanently under white control.

Officially, nobody could now stop blacks voting simply because they were black. But blacks had to join a register of voters before each election, and the whites could say that people were not allowed to register if, for example, they could not read. Reading tests were introduced, but whites were often allowed to learn the test by heart in advance. Marriages were not allowed between people of different races. Blacks were not allowed to give evidence in court against whites or to sit on juries — especially if a white man was on trial. Because of this, it was very unlikely that a white man in the South could ever be found guilty of a crime against a black man, because the black man would be unable to find people to back up his story, or a jury that would believe him.

A new series of laws between 1865 and 1907 also enforced segregation. Blacks had to be kept apart from whites in schools, houses, trains and buses, restaurants — even in jails, hospitals and homes for the blind. Blacks were often not allowed to join unions, and negro unemployment was always very high. Blacks appealed to the American government but were told that although negroes must be allowed their rights, segregation in schools and jobs was allowed as long as each race had equal opportunities. In fact, the opportunities were far from equal. By the 1930s, Southern states spent four times as much on educating a white child as a black one.

At the same time a very unpleasant secret society grew up in the South — the Ku Klux Klan. Only whites could join; they performed strange ceremonies in white hoods, often at night, so that nobody could tell exactly who they were. Their main aim was to make people think that blacks were evil, and to make negroes so frightened that they would not dare to challenge what the white state governments were doing. Many blacks

were beaten up or even killed by members of the Klan. This was the atmosphere in the South when Martin Luther King was born on 15 January 1929.

There were no segregation laws in the Northern states because with fewer blacks in that area, there was no need for them. But in practice the situation was much the same, with blacks forced to accept the lowest-paid jobs and the worst housing.

In the South many people got so used to being badly treated that they began to believe whites really were superior to them. But others, like Daddy King, believed this simply was not true, and that if only blacks were treated fairly they would be able to show what they could achieve. Blacks needed to win their civil rights, their rights as citizens, to vote, to mix freely with whites in public places and to have equal opportunities in housing and jobs. The problem was — how could they win those civil rights?

3 The most peculiar child

Compared with many blacks in Atlanta in the 1930s, the King family was well-off. They owned a large house in a pleasant part of the town, and had plenty of food and clothes. Daddy King was proud of not having to depend on other people. 'We've never lived in a rented home and never had a car long on which payment was due,' he said.

The family was a happy one. Martin's mother was kind and calm; she always thought carefully before she spoke. The three children, Christine, Martin and Alfred Daniel ('A.D.') loved their father, although Martin in particular found him difficult at times. Daddy King wanted Martin to become a preacher like himself. Martin was not at all sure about it and he wanted to plan his own life. When Daddy King insisted on something unpopular, Christine would usually give in, A.D. would openly resist and Martin, firm but polite, would listen quietly and then go off and make his own decision. He could be extremely stubborn. 'He was the most peculiar child whenever you whipped him,' said his father. 'He'd stand there and the tears would run down. But he would never cry.'

Like many boys, Martin smoked his first cigarette behind a fence and had a succession of girl friends. He loved playing football and baseball and he was a good tennis player. He did a regular paper round, and spent much of his earnings on smart clothes. Throughout his life he loved good suits and shoes, and some people nicknamed him 'Tweed' because of this.

Although he often got into rough-and-tumble wrestling contests with other black boys, he disliked hitting people and always avoided fights. But occasionally his anger boiled over. Once, when A.D. teased Christine until she cried, Martin smashed him on the head with a telephone. 'He almost knocked my brains out,' said A.D. But as he got older, Martin disliked violence more and more. When the school bully, 'Black Billy', kicked him all the way downstairs, he did not fight back at all.

Martin preferred talking to fighting. 'Even before he could read, he kept books around him,' said Daddy King. He became fascinated by long words, and learned that words could be used to influence and persuade people. After listening to a particularly good preacher one Sunday, he told his mother 'Some day I'm going to have me some big words like that'. He was right.

As he grew older, he put his words to good use and became a skilled debater. One night, as his team came back from a debate ninety miles from Atlanta, the bus driver ordered them to give up their seats to white people and called them 'Black sons of bitches'. Their Black teacher told them that it was better to obey the law than to resist, and they had to stand all the way. Martin remembered: 'It was a night I'll never forget. I don't think I have ever been so angry in my life.'

At the age of fifteen, he won a place at Daddy King's old college, Morehouse, on a special course for gifted black students. He still had no plans to become a minister like his father because he felt that it was not a job for someone with a really good brain. He did not like all the shouting and clapping in negro churches. He felt he could do more to help his fellow-blacks if he became a doctor or perhaps a lawyer.

In college holidays he took temporary jobs. He noticed that blacks were always paid less than whites for doing the same work. He gave up a railway job when the foreman refused to stop calling him 'Nigger', and he travelled to the North to work on a farm. Although he found many blacks there as poor as those in Atlanta, the laws in the North did not stop him travelling and eating with whites. On the train home it came as a great shock when he had to eat behind a curtain in the dining car. 'I felt as if a curtain had been dropped on my manhood,' he said.

Slowly he grew more and more interested in becoming a preacher. He and the other students were especially impressed by the Tuesday morning sermons of the college president, Dr Benjamin Mays, about the need to change Southern society. Perhaps preaching could help to change things after all. At the age of seventeen he preached a brilliantly successful trial sermon in his father's church. Two years later, in June 1948, he left Morehouse as a Baptist minister with the highest marks in his exams. It was time to continue his education in the North.

4 A very bright young man

Crozer College near Philadelphia was nearly a thousand kilometres north of Atlanta. It drew both black and white students from all over the United States. Martin studied there from 1948 until 1951, learning religious ideas and church history. His teachers were most impressed by his hard work. 'A very bright young man. He seems to know where he wants to go and how to get there,' observed one of them.

Martin was deeply influenced by the works of two men: Walter Rauschenbusch and Mahatma Gandhi. Rauschenbusch had written that religious people should not only try to improve men's souls and thoughts, but also to make their everyday lives happier and fairer. Gandhi's ideas were even more important to him. This great Indian religious leader had led his people to freedom from British rule in 1947 without firing a single bullet or speaking a violent word. Gandhi believed that the way to protest against injustice in society was not by violent actions but by setting an example of peacefulness and love. Like Christ, Gandhi had preached peace and yet had been killed himself. (He was shot in 1948.) Martin now decided that non-violence was the way to change American society too.

Martin also seems to have had time to meet plenty of girls. He fell briefly in love with a white girl, but knew that in those days a mixed marriage would have caused a terrible scandal. On his last day at Crozer several girls phoned the college, all asking if they could come to watch Martin receive his Bachelor of Divinity degree.

The Indian religious leader, Mahatma Gandhi, had a great influence on Martin

Each of them pretended to be engaged to him!

He also liked his food. 'He could eat more than any little man you ever saw in your life,' said one friend, and Martin admitted that 'Eating is my great sin'. Once his appetite nearly got him into serious trouble. Although Philadelphia officially banned the segregation of restaurants, in practice blacks still ate separately from whites, in their own areas of each town. One day, Martin, a friend and two girls went into a restaurant. The owner refused to give them a menu and asked them to leave. They refused and he drew a pistol. Finally they left, afraid of the danger to the girls.

But later on Martin went back to the restaurant with a policeman. He persuaded three white people who had seen what happened to support him. But when the case came to court, all three refused to give evidence and pretended that they had forgotten what they saw. Once again, Martin learned how much negroes had to suffer, even when the law seemed to support them.

On another occasion a white Southern student at Crozer threatened to shoot him. The man accused Martin of overturning the furniture in his college room, even though there was absolutely no evidence that Martin had been near it. The other students pointed out what a terrible thing such an accusation was, and the man apologised. He and Martin later became friends.

Martin left Crozer as its most outstanding student, with a major scholarship to study at any American university. He then travelled still further north, to the University of Boston. He worked there for his Doctor of Philosophy degree and his flat became a centre for other black students who wanted to meet and exchange ideas. While he was in Boston, he also met Coretta Scott, the girl who was to become his wife.

Coretta Scott came from another Southern state, Alabama. Blacks were treated very badly there, too. Her family had managed to get a small plot of land, from which her father eventually made enough money to buy a small saw-mill, despite the opposition of a white man who wanted to buy it himself. Soon afterwards, the mill mysteriously burned down. But Obadiah Scott started again with great determination and within a few years he owned a petrol station and several other small businesses.

Coretta was also a very determined person. Martin, who was proud of his success with girls, liked the sound of her and rang her up. Although he had never met her, he clearly expected to sweep her off her feet. 'I am like Napoleon at Waterloo before your charms,' he complimented her down the phone. 'That's absurd,' she replied, 'you haven't even seen me yet.' But at the end of their first meeting Martin told her 'You have all the qualities that I expect to find in the girl I'd like to have for a wife'.

Coretta thought carefully about marrying Martin during the summer of 1952. 'The more I saw of him, the more I liked him,' she remembers. But becoming a minister's wife would mean giving up the career she had planned as a concert singer. Finally, she said yes to him. Daddy King, who still wanted to plan Martin's life for him, objected at first. He hoped Martin would

Coretta Scott, who later became Martin's wife

come back to Atlanta to work with him, and he had found a local girl whom he hoped to have as a daughter-in-law. But he soon gave in, and conducted the marriage service at the Scotts' home in June 1953.

Martin wondered where he should take charge of his first church. Plenty of churches wanted this promising student. A Northern town seemed attractive; educated blacks were treated better there. But he and Coretta decided that they had a duty to return to the South and to work for people there — not in Atlanta, but at the Dexter Avenue Baptist Church in Montgomery, the state capital of Alabama.

Fifteen happy and peaceful months followed. Martin finished his studies. Coretta gave birth to a baby girl. Martin thought he might preach and write for a few years and then perhaps become a college professor. But he had reckoned without the case of Rosa Parks.

5 'Tired of being kicked about'

On Thursday 1 December 1955 a white Montgomery bus driver ordered Mrs Rosa Parks to give up her seat to a white passenger. Mrs Parks refused — she was old and had just finished a hard day's work. 'I was just plain tired, and my feet hurt,' she explained later. Although the driver did not know Mrs Parks, who was highly respected in the black community, her quiet and polite determination made him realise that he wasn't dealing simply with a woman who was mad or drunk. Some drivers would have thrown her forcibly off the bus — one or two blacks had even been killed in such incidents in the past — but driver Blake thought this would embarrass the white passengers, so he called the police.

The other black people on the bus did nothing. They had become so used to this sort of discrimination that they could see no point in fighting it. But news of Mrs Parks's arrest spread like wildfire through the black districts. A local civil rights worker, E. D. Nixon, went to the police station and arranged for her release, even though he was told there that 'this nigger is none of your God-damned business'. On the way home, Nixon persuaded Mrs Parks that the time had come to draw attention to the suffering of all Montgomery's blacks by making her arrest the cause of a major protest. 'She was anchored to that seat,' wrote Martin, 'by all the indignities of days gone by and by the boundless hopes of generations yet unborn.' But if Mrs Parks was not the first person to be arrested for refusing to give up a bus

The fingerprinting of Rosa Parks, who refused to give up her seat to a white passenger

seat, why should her arrest trigger such a protest?

The negroes were already bitterly resentful about the unfair trial of a black man who had recently been accused of attacking a white woman. On the other hand, some help for Southern blacks did seem to be at last on the way. A year earlier the United States Supreme Court — the highest legal body in America — had ruled that school segregation in another Southern town, Little Rock in Arkansas, was illegal. The American government in Washington had recently banned segregation on buses travelling between one state and another. A demonstration now might help to speed up further reform.

Nixon phoned a number of black leaders in Montgomery to tell them of Mrs Parks's arrest. He asked Martin to join a committee to organise a boycott of the buses — to persuade all blacks to refuse to use them. Martin liked the idea, but asked for time to think about it. He had only recently arrived in the town and felt that church work must be his first priority. His baby daughter was only a few weeks old. He had doubts about whether his fellow black ministers or the blacks in general would have enough determination to carry on a long boycott. But Mrs Parks's own minister, the Reverend Ralph Abernathy, persuaded him. Ralph

With the Reverend Ralph Abernathy (*left*) who became one of Martin's closest friends and supporters

was a forceful man, less cautious than Martin, who now became one of his closest friends and supporters.

40,000 leaflets were sent out, urging blacks to boycott the buses from Monday, 5 December. 'If you work,' they said, 'take a taxi, or share a ride, or walk. Come to a mass meeting on Monday at 7 p.m. for further instructions.' Meanwhile, Martin and Ralph organised a meeting of local black ministers at Martin's church.

The meeting was rather chaotic. Nixon was not there, as he had to work his shift on the railways. In his absence, there was no obvious leader. But the ministers all agreed on the boycott and drew up detailed plans. Black taxi drivers agreed to charge people only the normal bus fare.

When Martin drove round the city on the day the boycott started, he estimated that there were less than a dozen negroes on the buses. Rosa Parks was fined $10 for her 'offence'. In the afternoon the Montgomery Improvement Association (MIA) came into being, aiming to improve things for the blacks in all areas of life where they were treated differently from whites. Martin was elected president. 'It happened so quickly that I didn't even have time to think it through,' he said. The main reason why he was chosen was that more and more people could see his wisdom and qualities of leadership. There was also the fact that, as a minister, he could find a job in another city more easily than many blacks if the boycott failed.

That evening he spoke to a meeting of more than 4,000 people. They heard a prayer, a bible reading and then Martin's speech. 'We are tired of being segregated and humiliated, tired of being kicked about . . . we have no alternative but to protest. We have been amazingly patient. But we have come here tonight for freedom and justice,' he proclaimed. 'The Ku Klux Klan are protesting for the perpetuation of injustice. We're protesting for the birth of justice. We will be guided by the highest principles of law and order. If you will protest courageously and yet with dignity and Christian love, future historians will say "There lived a great people — a black people — who injected new meaning and dignity into the veins of our civilisation".' The meeting agreed to continue the boycott until the blacks won equal treatment on the buses. A pool of 300 cars was set up; blacks with cars would give lifts wherever possible to those who would otherwise have to walk.

'After ascending the mountain on Monday night, I woke up on Tuesday morning, urgently aware that I had to come back to earth,' wrote Martin. He was now a leader. But he would also be a marked man, a target for fierce white hatred.

6 God spoke from Washington

Martin did not have long to wait before his worst fears were realised. He and other MIA leaders received a stream of hateful and threatening phone calls. One caller said 'Listen nigger. Before next week you'll be sorry that you ever came to Montgomery.' Martin was arrested and put into the city jail for driving at just over the speed limit. Only the arrival of a large, angry crowd persuaded the police to release him. When he made a brief visit home to Atlanta, Daddy King and other leaders there tried to persuade him not to go back because the situation was so dangerous. Martin felt it was his duty to return, although he now reluctantly carried a pistol because there were rumours of a plot to kill him.

Three weeks earlier, his house had been bombed. Martin had been out, but Coretta and a friend were there, and the baby was asleep upstairs. Something like a brick was tossed into the porch and there was a huge explosion which shattered windows and filled the downstairs rooms with smoke. Then the telephone rang. Coretta answered it. A woman's voice said, 'I did it. And I'm just sorry I didn't kill all you bastards.' Fortunately, nobody was harmed.

Martin rushed home. An angry group of blacks had gathered outside. The situation was turning nasty. He heard one man yelling at a policeman: 'You white folks is always pushing us around. You've got your gun and I've got mine, so let's battle it out.' After making sure that Coretta and the baby were all right, Martin called

Being arrested for a driving offence

for quiet. His words showed what he had learned from his Christian faith and Gandhi's writings. 'Don't get your weapons. He who lives by the sword will perish by the sword. Remember, that is what God said. We do not want violence. We want to love our enemies. We must love our white brothers, no matter what they do to us.' The crowd, now quiet, chanted 'Amen' and went home. One policeman admitted 'If it hadn't been for that nigger preacher, we'd all be dead.'

Money began pouring in to the MIA from all over the world. But the boycott — and Martin's problems — went on. He was arrested and fined $10 on a trumped-up charge of refusing to obey a policeman. The whites who ran the city and the bus company were determined to break the boycott. They tried to spread rumours that some blacks were ready to give in. They hinted that MIA leaders were keeping some of the gifts of money for themselves and that Martin had bought himself a car in this way. They also found an old state law forbidding boycotts. Martin and others were found guilty of breaking this law; he was fined another $500. Then the whites tried to get a court order banning the car pool. If they succeeded, Martin was afraid the court might order him and his followers to pay the $15,000 which the city claimed to have lost because of the boycott. He knew they would not be able to pay.

He also felt that as winter came round again, people would be less willing to walk to work. During the summer they gladly supported the boycott: 'It used to be my soul that was tired and my feet that was rested. Now my feets are tired but my soul is rested,' one old black woman told a reporter. But would she still feel the same way when summer was over?

When Martin learned that the car pool hearing would be conducted by the same judge who had fined him earlier in the year, all hope seemed lost. But as he sat in the courtroom, a reporter handed him a note. The Supreme Court in Washington had just ruled that Alabama's bus segregation was against American law. Nothing that Montgomery's whites might do could alter that verdict. 'God Almighty has spoken from Washington D.C.' cried one old man. 'God decided to use Montgomery as the proving ground for the struggle and triumph of freedom and justice in America,' declared Martin. 'This is not a victory for negroes alone, but for all Montgomery and the South.'

The MIA called off the boycott after just over a year. Its leaders asked blacks not to reply or hit back if they were insulted, nor to boast or gloat about their victory, and not to sit next to whites on buses if other seats were free. They hoped everyone would thus slowly accept desegregation. They were disappointed. Some whites did everything they could to pick fights with negroes; buses were shot at; someone tried again to bomb Martin's house. But eventually the violence died away.

Martin had won his first great victory. He took one of the first buses of the day on 21 December 1956 and sat next to a white minister from New York. He rode round the city for some hours to see that there was no trouble as the boycott ended. Segregation had suffered a major defeat. But there was still a great deal of work to be done.

7 The time has come

Between 1957 and 1962 Martin's fame spread across the world. Newspapers and magazines in many countries wrote articles about him, and he wrote his first book called *Stride towards Freedom*. He made hundreds of speeches and travelled widely. One visit was specially important to him — his journey to the country of Mahatma Gandhi. 'To other countries I may go as a tourist,' he said, 'but to India I come as a pilgrim.' He came home more convinced than ever that every man had the right to resist laws that were unjust and inhuman — as long as he resisted without violence.

Martin also helped to set up the Southern Leadership Christian Conference (SCLC). This group included many Southern black ministers who were now fighting for civil rights in their own towns and cities. Martin became president of SCLC and set up its headquarters at Atlanta. He hoped that from now on all the attempts to change society could be drawn together.

In 1957 SCLC announced a 'Call to the nation'. A mass meeting would be held at the memorial to President Abraham Lincoln in the centre of Washington on 17 May. The meeting was to be non-violent and religious in style. Southern blacks would play the major part, but Martin hoped also to attract negroes from the poorest city areas in the North, and whites who supported his cause.

Some black leaders hoped there would be over 50,000 people there. They estimated the actual crowd to be 37,000, although local police said 15,000 was a more

'Freedom Riders' being arrested at the bus terminal

accurate figure. Some employers ordered their black workers to stay at work as it was a weekday; only a very few whites attended. But despite these disappointments, Martin made a powerful speech. 'Give us the vote,' he declared, 'and we will put judges in the South who will give us justice and mercy.'

The meeting did achieve one important aim. President Eisenhower agreed to meet Martin and other negro leaders at the White House. There they pleaded for real voting rights and for police protection against the bombing of black homes and churches. The President was sympathetic, but he made no firm promises.

Martin's own work came to a dramatic halt for a time in 1958. On 20 September he was signing copies of his book in a New York department store when a large negro woman, Izola Curry, pushed her way to the front of the crowd. 'Luther King, I have been after you for five years!' she cried, and plunged a long letter-opener into his chest. Martin was amazingly calm; he just sat still while store officials stopped hysterical women from trying to pull the dagger out. It was just as well that they did. It took surgeons three hours to remove it, and they said afterwards that it had been so close to his heart that one sneeze or cough might have killed him.

Mrs Curry was put into a hospital for the criminally insane. Martin believed the stabbing was a symbol of the hatred and bitterness in American society. 'Today it was I,' he said. 'Tomorrow it could be another leader or any man.' He showed no hatred for his attacker, saying only that he hoped she might eventually be cured of her illness and then set free. But it was well into 1959 before he could start work again.

Violence was growing once more in the South. Many whites were determined not to give in to black pressure. Civil rights workers were beaten up. Black houses were bombed. A negro was hanged by an angry mob in Mississippi. Blacks replied with sit-ins and mass marches. Martin was worried because other leaders were beginning to preach about the need for 'Black Power', saying that only violence could bring about reform and that blacks needed their own separate state. As SCLC matters took up more and more of his time, he could not attend fully to his church congregation in Montgomery.

He preached to a packed church there on 29 November 1959. 'For about five years now,' he told them, 'I have been trying to do what five or six people ought to be doing. I have to reorganise my life. History has thrust something upon me which I cannot turn away.' And so, with great regret, he resigned as their minister. From now on he would assist his father at his church in Atlanta whenever he had no other engagements. His congregation joined hands and sang one of the old slave songs. Martin broke down in tears in the pulpit.

In 1960, though, black students all over the South began sit-ins at lunch counters and restaurants to end segregation there. Martin was sitting with a group of them in an Atlanta store when the police arrested them all. Six months earlier he had been found guilty of a very minor traffic offence and fined $25. He had been told then that he would go to jail if he broke the law again during the next twelve months. Now the police saw their chance. Martin was sentenced to six months in a distant jail where black prisoners were always treated very badly. Coretta was expecting another baby, so visits would not be easy. It was only when John F. Kennedy, then trying to win election as President, put pressure on government officials in Washington that Martin was released. At this time he was also accused of making false tax statements. To be called dishonest hurt him very deeply, and he was delighted when a white jury found him not guilty.

Then black students devised a new type of protest, the 'Freedom Ride'. Groups travelled on buses through the South, ignoring the segregation laws in bus stations and restaurants on the way. Many were arrested or beaten up, and some blacks began to criticise Martin's leadership. Why hadn't he gone on a freedom ride himself? He had always said he was ready to go to jail, so why had he suddenly allowed Kennedy to rescue him? Hadn't Kennedy simply used him to win black votes? Was non-violence really the way to win reform?

All these doubts helped to cause Martin's greatest failure — the campaign in Albany, Georgia in 1961-2. When freedom riders were arrested there, Martin organised a march to the city hall. Sit-ins and boycotts followed for four months, but victory did not come here as it had done in Montgomery. The local leadership was poorly organised, and some ministers thought that Martin was a trouble-making outsider, making matters worse. Some disliked the fact that he was now directly encouraging people to break the law. The white authorities did not make the same mistake as those in Montgomery, either. The police stayed calm and made few arrests. On television it therefore looked to many viewers as if the blacks were the ones in the wrong. Kennedy, now President, had other urgent problems, so when Martin planned another march, Washington supported the Albany authorities when they banned it.

The Albany failure taught Martin not to under-estimate his enemies. 1957-62 had been a difficult time. Now he was preparing for an even tougher campaign — in Birmingham, Alabama.

8 Justice too long delayed

In January 1963 Martin met President Kennedy and pleaded for new civil rights laws within months which would apply to every American state. Kennedy was impressed, but said action could not be taken so quickly. Disappointed, Martin told the President that he would soon be launching a new campaign in Birmingham, Alabama.

The campaign was very carefully planned. The timing was important; Martin felt that without another major victory soon, his supporters might turn to violence. The movement might even collapse. The place was deliberately chosen. Martin described Birmingham as 'the most thoroughly segregated city in America'. Negro property had been attacked seventeen times in five years; whites had killed blacks and got off scot-free. Less than a quarter of the blacks were registered to vote, and blacks had the worst housing. Jobs were scarce. Alabama's governor, George Wallace, had the slogan 'Segregation for ever!' Birmingham's mayor, Arthur Hanes, called Martin a 'revolutionary nigger-king'. Police Commissioner Eugene 'Bull' Connor had a reputation for cruelty. 'I may not be able to enforce segregation,' he used to say, 'but I'll die trying.'

Martin went to Birmingham several times to check that black leaders there supported him fully and that everything was organised. Money was raised to pay the legal costs of anyone arrested. Definite aims were agreed — the desegregation of restaurants and more jobs for blacks in city stores. The campaign began on

3 April 1963 with a series of small sit-ins. Martin toured the city, persuading doubters to join in and insisting that everyone should promise to keep 'Ten Commandments' of non-violence.

The police made few arrests in the first four days. But on Sunday the 7th they waded into a crowd with sticks and dogs. The demonstrators were carried off to jail singing 'We shall overcome', which was now the battle song of the whole movement. The state court banned all future sit-ins, marches and boycotts.

On Good Friday, 12 April, Martin told a large crowd at Zion Hill church that things could be changed only if they were prepared to suffer. He led a march on the city hall. Blacks lined the streets shouting 'Freedom has come to Birmingham!'. Bull Connor allowed the marchers to set off, but then yelled to his policemen 'Stop 'em! Don't let 'em go any further.' Martin, Ralph and fifty-three others were thrown into jail, and Martin was not allowed to see anyone at all.

Although he was used to jail, Martin described the next few hours as 'the longest, most frustrating and bewildering I have lived. You will never know the meaning of utter darkness until you have lain in such a dungeon, knowing that light is streaming overhead, and seeing only darkness below'. He was desperately worried. Would the protest collapse without him? Coretta had just had another child, but he was not allowed to speak even to her. She did not know if he was alive. After two days she decided only one man could help — the President. She managed to contact him, and fifteen minutes later Martin was on the phone to her.

He used his eight days in prison well, writing his famous *Letter from Birmingham Jail*. This was especially for local white ministers who thought that he had no business creating trouble in Birmingham. He told them that local black leaders had asked him to come, and that unjust laws must sometimes be broken. He gave them an example: strictly speaking, it had been 'illegal' for Germans to resist Hitler, but surely it had been right? 'We have waited more than 340 years for our rights,' he told them.

As soon as he was freed, he and other leaders drew up a new plan. Adult support was not strong enough, so they would call on Birmingham's black schoolchildren to join in. It was a very hard decision to take because nobody knew what the police might do to child demonstrators. On 2 May thousands of young blacks marched through the city singing 'We shall overcome'. Black schools were almost empty next day as even more children gathered to repeat the march, chanting 'We want freedom!' The police ordered them to stop and then charged with sticks and hoses. The water pressure knocked some children over and ripped clothes off others. When bottles and bricks were thrown at the police, Connor released his dogs. 'Look at those niggers run', he yelled.

But Martin had forecast correctly what would happen now. The demonstrations went on. By the end of a week, the prisons were overflowing. As the police began to realise that there was nothing they could do, they became more violent. Television and newspaper pictures of the police attacks on children were seen in

Firemen direct a stream of water to break up the demonstration by hundreds of negroes in Birmingham, Alabama

every home in America and abroad, and thousands of people protested to Washington about what was going on. There was so much sympathy for the black cause that President Kennedy had to send a representative to Birmingham to arrange peace talks. 'Bull Connor has done as much for civil rights as Abraham Lincoln,' declared Kennedy.

At first, white leaders refused to talk. But they soon came to realise that they could not fight this movement as the demonstrators refused to use violence. On 10 May they agreed to desegregate many public places and to drop charges against the demonstrators.

'As Birmingham goes, so goes the South,' Martin had

predicted at the start of the campaign. He was right. Victory at Birmingham was a huge blow against discrimination in every Southern state. There was a brief bout of violence when negroes stoned police and set fire to buildings after A. D. King's home was bombed. There was also a terrible tragedy six months later, when four little black girls were killed by a bomb in the same Birmingham church from which the marchers had set out. But after Birmingham, the South could never go back to its old ways. A great victory had been won. Now Martin planned another massive meeting in Washington itself. It would be remembered as the highpoint of his life's work.

9 I have a dream

Martin Luther King was now at the peak of his career. In towns and cities across America, negroes began to copy the tactics he had used in Birmingham, staging their own marches and sit-ins, singing the same freedom songs. Martin himself made a triumphant speaking tour. 25,000 came to hear him in Los Angeles, 10,000 in Chicago. He led 125,000 on an amazing 'Freedom Walk' in Detroit.

Whites as well as blacks had begun to take notice of Martin's call to put right whatever was wrong or unjust in America's way of life. Most important of all, President Kennedy realised that he should now give his full support to the movement. He was the first American President to say that segregation was morally wrong, and he urged business, trades union and white church leaders to work actively for a fairer society. In an important speech in June 1963, he spoke words which Martin would have been proud to say himself:

> 'One hundred years of delay have passed since President Lincoln freed the slaves, yet their grandsons are not truly free from social and economic oppression. Now the time has come for this nation to fulfil its promise. The events in Birmingham and elsewhere have so increased the cries for equality that no city or state can choose to ignore them . . .'

Two months later, on 28 August 1963, Martin organised the event at which he made the greatest speech of his life. In a repeat of the 'Prayer Pilgrimage'

Martin made the greatest speech of his life at the Lincoln Memorial in Washington

of 1957, he staged a march on the Lincoln Memorial in Washington. This time there were no disappointments. 250,000 men and women came from all over America, and no less than a quarter of them were white. It was the largest civil rights demonstration in American history. When Martin rose to speak, the crowd fell totally silent.

At first, he read from a prepared speech. Echoing President Kennedy's words, he stressed that although slavery had officially ended a century earlier, black Americans were still not truly free. He appealed to whites to support him. 'With our white brothers . . . we shall march ahead. We cannot turn back. We shall never be satisfied as long as a negro in Mississippi cannot vote and a negro in New York believes he has nothing for which to vote. Go back to Mississippi; go back to Alabama. Go back to Georgia; go back to Louisiana. Go back to the slums and ghettoes of our Northern cities knowing that somehow this situation can, and will, be changed.'

Then he began to speak words which had not been fully prepared in advance. Over and over again he used the phrase 'I have a dream'. Each time he said it, the crowd urged him on.

'I have a dream that one day on the red hills of Georgia the sons of former slaves and the sons of former slave owners will be able to sit down together at the table of brotherhood. I have a dream that one day even the state of Mississippi . . . will be transformed into an oasis of freedom and justice.

I have a dream that one day my four little children will live in a nation where they will not be judged by the colour of their skin but by the content of their character . . . where little black boys and little white boys will be able to join hands and walk together as brothers.

This will be the day when all of God's children will be able to sing with new meaning "Let Freedom ring!" When we allow freedom to ring from every town and every hamlet, from every state and every city, we will be able to speed up that day when all God's children, black men and white men, will be able to join hands and sing in the words of the old negro spiritual "Free at last, Free at last. Great God A'mighty, I'm free at last!"'

As he ended, there was a brief silence. Then suddenly the crowd began to shout his words back at him over and over again. As Coretta said, 'They kept on shouting in one thunderous voice, and for that brief moment the Kingdom of God seemed to have come on earth.'

10 We must stand up

Martin's year of triumph, 1963, ended tragically. In November President John Kennedy was shot dead in Dallas, Texas. Martin had come to have a great respect for Kennedy, and he was one of 1,200 people invited to the funeral in Washington. As he sat in the cathedral with kings and queens, presidents and prime ministers from around the world, he was desperately sad. Kennedy's death showed him, just like the deaths of civil rights workers or those little girls in the Birmingham church bombing, that America had what he called 'an atmosphere in which violence and hatred have become popular pastimes'. He was also fearful. 'This is what is going to happen to me,' he told Coretta.

He worked so hard in 1964 that he had to go into hospital to rest. While he was away from home, Coretta received a phone call. Martin had won the Nobel Prize for Peace, perhaps the most highly respected award in the world, for his struggle for civil rights and, above all, for his insistence on non-violent methods. The Kings travelled to Oslo, Norway, to receive the award. Martin gave away the $54,600 prize money to the freedom movement. On the way there, he stopped in London and preached to 4,000 people in St Paul's Cathedral.

The new President, Lyndon B. Johnson, invited Martin to the White House to watch him sign the 1964 Civil Rights Act. Kennedy had been working on this law when he died. It banned discrimination in any organisation which received money from the American

Receiving the Nobel Peace Prize from Gunnar John, the chairman of the Nobel Prize Committee

government. Now Martin decided to concentrate his work on stopping blacks being threatened with violence if they tried to register as voters. In Alabama only 25 per cent of those blacks entitled to vote were actually on the voters' list; in the town of Selma only 1 in 50 of them actually voted.

On 1 February 1965 Martin led a great demonstration to the Selma courthouse. He and more than a thousand people were arrested, many of them schoolchildren. 'There's going to be some niggers killed like flies before this is over,' predicted a white garage mechanic who watched the marchers go by. Meanwhile another negro leader, Malcolm X, arrived. His message was quite different from Martin's — that violence was the only way to win reforms. Although Malcolm X assured Coretta that he had come to support Martin's efforts, his presence made Martin even more fearful that things might get out of control.

After his release on 5 February, Martin urged the President to introduce a Voting Rights bill with government inspectors to make sure that there were no threats when blacks registered to vote. He organised more marches. 'My voice is almost gone,' he croaked, 'but my feet are in time.' Soon the campaign suffered its first casualty. Police suddenly switched off the street lights during a demonstration at night, and a black man was gunned down.

Martin then decided on a great march from Selma to Montgomery, Alabama's state capital. 'I can't promise you that you won't get beaten or your house bombed,' he told his followers. 'But we must stand up for what is right.' Alabama's governor George Wallace banned the march, but 500 blacks set out on Sunday 7 March, only to be brutally beaten up by the police with guns, whips and tear-gas.

Martin prepared for a new march two days later. This time, the Washington government banned it. Martin reluctantly decided to ignore this ban, too, and asked the whole nation for support. 1,500 people set out with him, half of them white. When they met the police, they knelt down in prayer. Then Martin ordered them all to turn back. He was fiercely criticised for doing so. One Black Power leader said 'Martin denied history a great moment, never to be recaptured'. He thought a

A happy moment for the Kings as they rejoin the Selma to Montgomery march

really violent confrontation would have forced Washington to take action. Martin may have feared that Ku Klux Klan rifle snipers were hidden along the route. He probably feared offending the Washington government, which seemed now much more helpful than in earlier years. Whatever the reason, his followers were very surprised and disheartened.

But white extremists now made a huge mistake. James Reeb was a white minister who had come down from the North to support Martin. When whites saw him coming out of a black restaurant after the march, they smashed his skull. Reeb's death led to demonstrations all over the country. Twelve students held a sit-in at the White House itself. President Johnson promised that there would be a voting rights law. Governor Wallace tried to persuade him that the violence was all due to revolutionary troublemakers, but Johnson was in no mood to listen. 'I think all of us realise that there is much that should have been done that has not been done,' he said. 'What happened in Selma is the effort of American negroes to secure for themselves the full blessings of American life. Their cause must be our cause, too. We *shall* overcome.' Martin described the speech as 'one of the most passionate pleas for human rights ever made by a President of the United States'.

President Johnson sent government troops to protect the marchers. 'Walk together, children; don't you get weary and it will lead us to the Promised Land,' Martin told his followers. 'And Alabama will be a new Alabama, and America will be a new America.' Nearly 30,000 people marched the last five kilometres into Montgomery.

When a white mother of five children was gunned down by furious white extremists as she gave a black man a lift back to the North in her car, America was horrified. That same year, the Voting Rights Bill became law. As Coretta listened to Martin's victory speech in Montgomery, she realised 'we had come a long way from our start in the bus protest in 1957 when only a handful of people were involved'.

11 I've seen the Promised Land

In many ways, the final period of Martin's life was the most difficult one. The more he achieved, the more his followers expected. Their hopes were not always realised, and some turned on him bitterly. The more famous he became, the more Martin felt he must speak out on all the great problems of his day. This made him unpopular, too. Some people felt that he was getting too self-important, and they nicknamed him 'De Lawd'. They said that if he got involved in other issues, it would take attention away from the Civil Rights movement.

They were especially concerned when Martin spoke out against the Vietnam war. During the 1960s America was sending more and more troops there to stop the spread of Communism. Many Americans felt that the United States had no business to fight a war thousands of kilometres across the Pacific Ocean, and they were angry about the suffering and loss of life it caused. There were violent protests all across the country. Martin, supported by Coretta, declared that war was always wrong. 'It is sinful for any of God's children to brutalise any of God's other children,' he said. This view lost him the support of other Americans who thought that the war was right and that Martin was being unpatriotic and interfering. President Johnson certainly thought so. Martin could expect much less help from the government now.

He was also getting worried about the spread of Black Power ideas. After vicious race riots in the

The last family photo, Christmas 1966

Western city of Los Angeles in 1965, he toured the ruined houses. 'We won, we won!' boasted a group of blacks. 'How can you say you won when thirty-four negroes are dead, your community is destroyed and whites are using the riots as an excuse for inaction?' asked Martin. 'We won because we made them pay attention to us,' they retorted.

Martin was shocked that many of the blacks here had never heard of him or his work. All his efforts had been devoted to winning civil rights in the South. Now he must start fighting against the poverty, unemployment and poor housing that made life miserable in cities right across the nation. Otherwise, blacks would turn to violence as the only way to achieve change.

Early in 1966 he decided that Chicago, a Northern city, should be his new base. The SCLC opened an office there, and Martin and his family spent the summer living in a very poor little flat. He taught his neighbours to look after their streets and houses better. He got them to organise themselves into an army of occupiers who would refuse to pay rent until the landlords improved their houses as the law required.

In the summer of 1966 he organised a rally for over 50,000 people in Chicago. Again he preached that rioting would achieve nothing, and he demanded better housing, more jobs and equal opportunities for blacks in the city. The campaign went on all through that hot summer. Tension rose between whites and blacks. Black Power leaders urged violence — some blacks stopped singing 'We shall overcome' and chanted instead 'We shall over-run'. Many whites began to fear that even a peaceful protest like Martin's was helping to make violence inevitable. They began to buy guns to protect themselves.

These were dark days for Martin. Mayor Richard Daley of Chicago was very powerful and was determined not to give in to what he saw as Martin's lawlessness. He did draw up a 'Summit Agreement' with Martin in August, which promised that the city would work towards ending discrimination and helping blacks to get better housing. But the agreement was very vague and little was done. Action would have meant huge tax increases which white voters would not accept.

There were more race riots across America in 1967. Martin was sure that violence could be ended only if

Standing on the balcony (*centre*) of
the Memphis hotel the day before he was shot

there was a real attack on poverty. He decided that he must now fight for the poor of all races, not just the blacks. Early in 1968 he toured the country, recruiting poor people for a great Poor People's march on Washington to plead for help. His preaching became more urgent; he seemed to sense that he might not live long. 'The quality, not the length, of one's life is what is important,' he declared, and he told his staff that whatever happened to him, the work must go on.

In March 1968 he interrupted his Washington plans to lead a protest at Memphis, Tennessee, against police brutality during a demonstration by dustmen for higher pay. Black power agitators again stirred up violence.

On 3 April Martin spoke to a crowd there. 'I don't know what will happen to me now, but it really doesn't matter . . . I don't mind. Like anybody, I'd like to live a long life. But I just want to do God's will. And He's allowed me to go up to the mountain. And I've looked over and I've seen the Promised Land.'

The next evening he was standing on his motel balcony with Ralph Abernathy. A white man, James Earl Ray, shot him dead from across the street.

12 A life serving others

Martin's funeral was held at Daddy King's church in Atlanta and was attended by the Vice President and over eighty members of the American Congress. After a second service at Morehouse College, he was buried. On his marble monument are the words 'Free at last, free at last, thank God Almighty I'm free at last.'

But his work did not die with him. Coretta has done a great deal to publicise the problem of poverty, including leading protests against spending cuts by President Reagan's government. Ralph Abernathy and other black leaders have continued to work for civil rights by non-violent methods. When Martin's assassin (who was sentenced to ninety-nine years in jail) escaped in 1977, Daddy King said he would pray for his safety. He hoped the man would not be killed when the police recaptured him. Martin would have been proud of that response.

Violence did erupt in many American cities at the news of Martin's death, and has sometimes done so since. But much has been achieved for the American negro. Under Martin Luther King, segregation in the South became illegal, negroes gained the real right to vote and discrimination over housing and jobs was ended by law. By 1973 there were sixteen blacks in Congress. Within six years of that date, cities like Los Angeles and Detroit had elected black mayors. More surprisingly, even Southern cities like Atlanta, Birmingham and New Orleans had done the same. Under President Jimmy Carter (1977-81), blacks held

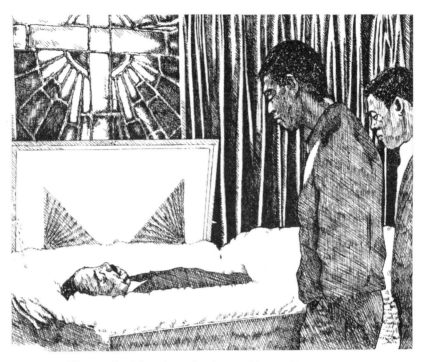

Thousands of Americans lined up to file past Martin's coffin

senior government posts, and at least ten served as ambassadors abroad and at the United Nations. More and more blacks have become lawyers, teachers, bankers, broadcasters and publishers — entering jobs which would have been unthinkable for them twenty years earlier. When ex-Governor George Wallace of Alabama, now confined to a wheelchair for life after an assassination attempt, stood for re-election as governor in 1982, many blacks actually voted for him, although Coretta King spoke strongly against him. He no longer preached segregation and they thought his government experience might help him to cut unemployment.

But a very great deal still remains to be done.

Although blacks now have the right to vote freely, by 1976 only half of them had registered to do so. Some black families are now rich, but a third of all blacks still live on or below the poverty line with barely enough food or clothing. Black slums in American cities are still among the worst in the world. Unemployment amongst blacks remains nearly twice as high as amongst whites.

So what sort of man was Martin Luther King? He was not a saint. He made decisions which some of his followers strongly disagreed with. Not all his campaigns were a success and he died before he had achieved all his aims. Some people thought that he was too much of an actor. He made enemies, notably the fanatically anti-Communist head of America's Intelligence network, J. Edgar Hoover. Hoover hated Martin because he believed any form of protest encouraged the spread of Communism. He did everything he could to destroy Martin's reputation.

But Martin Luther King was a man of tremendous courage and determination who was able to turn local protests into a nationwide crusade for justice. He was a man with a deep sense of what was right and wrong; a man who was prepared to suffer criticism, abuse, physical violence and eventually death, whilst preaching all the time that violence was evil; a man who started a movement for justice and equality and who achieved great results, although he died at the age of only thirty-nine.

Martin himself knew what he wanted history to say about him. He wanted to be seen as a 'drum-major' —

or leader — for justice, peace and righteousness.' He spoke once about the sort of funeral tribute he would like. There would be no need to mention the Nobel Prize or the 400 other awards. 'What's important is that Martin Luther King tried to give his life to serving others. That he tried to love somebody. I want you to be able to say that I did try to feed the hungry . . . to clothe the naked. And I want you to say that I tried to love and serve humanity.'

Martin Luther King did all these things. Others are still trying to do them. As Martin himself once said, quoting an old negro slave preacher: 'We ain't what we ought to be and we ain't what we want to be and we ain't what we're going to be. But, thank God, we ain't what we was.'